CONTENTS

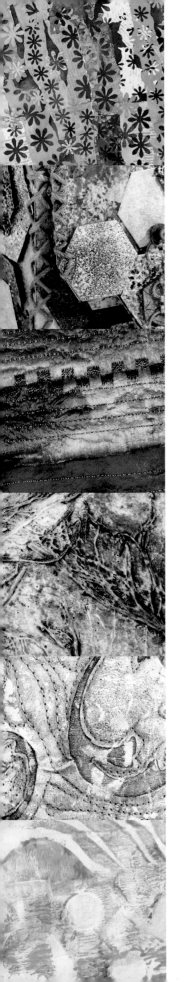

> Shrink plastic was die-cut, painted and shrunk using a heat tool. It was then decorated with metal shim and the inside pages were embossed with patterns. Jewellery rings were used to hold the book together. It is shown alongside a book made from an 'un-shrunk' version of the shape.

Introduction

I expect most of us have used cutting devices at some time and produced imaginative work with them. This book aims to bring together cutters of all descriptions, from simple shape punches to scanner or computer-controlled cutting devices that enable you to import your own designs. We concentrate our ideas most heavily around the die cutters, as they have so much to offer the textile artist. When combined with mixed media techniques and stitch, we found a huge variety of uses for a small number of dies.

The dies for the cutters have become larger and more inventive, some with motifs that link to a theme. These can be used for layered shapes in stitched quilts or wired motifs, or even set into gesso-painted backgrounds that resemble carved surfaces. These motifs are also suitable for three-dimensional work. One of the areas we found especially exciting here was the use of the negative shapes that remain when the cutting has taken place. We were so inspired that we built an entire section of this book around them.

The introduction of digital options, whether linked to a PC or a stand-alone scanner, opens new worlds of creativity. They give the freedom to use your own designs, and to see them transformed into perfectly cut shapes ready to be painted and/or stitched is magical.

We'd like to begin the book by telling you why we're all so hooked on cutting.

∧ Silk paper bowl with cut shapes trapped between the layers.

∨ This trial piece for a larger work was the catalyst for the use of gesso and wired shapes. When the cut shapes are coated with gesso and sprayed with ink, they resemble a carved surface, once gilded, now a sign of past glory.

Paula says, 'The moment I got my first die-cutting machine, my head began to buzz with ideas. Unfortunately I had only one die, a flower, but every time I used it with a different fabric or material, it opened more possibilities for use with textiles and mixed media work. Playing with layers, rotation, negative shapes, colour combinations and all kinds of materials was wonderful. I now have many dies but I still think that using each die to its full potential really gives so many ideas. You never know what's possible when you get a new shape, and I love to see other people discovering these possibilities for themselves.'

Sam says that she could see the possibilities in a die cutter as soon as she laid eyes on one: 'What really struck me was the way it took all the pain out of cutting multiple complex shapes. Who can cut the perfect circle, or cut a series of words for a textual piece, without feeling some disappointment in the end product? The sheer laboriousness of trying to cut out these shapes is made infinitely easier by the use of these dies. Having your shapes ready-cut does not signify a lack of imagination; it merely gives you more time and patience to use them to create something wonderful.'

Maggie says: 'I purchased a die-cutting machine so that I could use it as a press for collagraph prints. The thought of actually using it with dies didn't occur to me until I saw the work that Sam and Paula were producing, which prompted me to buy just two dies. I was instantly in love with the immediacy of the process, the options it offered and the different effects that I could achieve with my two dies, depending on the materials used with them. Having now purchased a few more dies, and also had some time to trial the digital versions, I feel my work will never be the same again.'

SECTION 1
Simple cutting ideas

Sometimes all you need for a great effect is a pair of scissors. I'm sure we've all enjoyed the children's paper-chain people, made from concertina folds and cut so that they all link together. Don't write them off as being too juvenile! Cut into more sophisticated shapes – they can be used for design work or made into stencils to be incorporated into fabric decoration.

∧ Free-cut paper feather stencils made by folding paper into quarters and cutting with a stylised feather shape. Red acrylic paint was applied with directional strokes.

< Free-cut feathers, made from tissue paper dress patterns and music sheets. These were bonded together with Heat'n'Bond to give strength and flexibility to the finely cut shapes.

< Jill Packer made this piece during a Sue Benner workshop by using a rotary cutter to cut strips and then bonding them to the background.

Rotary cutters

Rotary cutters can be exceptionally useful. It is possible to obtain fancy cutters to give a variety of shapes, as the work shown on this page demonstrates. Fine lines and shapely curves can be cut with ease, and a variety of blades and sizes are available, from scallop edges to those that merely perforate the fabric.

The colourful small quilt shown above was constructed using a rotary cutter to produce strips, which varied in shape and size. These were then bonded to a previously worked background fabric. This technique was studied at a Sue Benner workshop – for details, see inside back cover.

This bag was created with a rotary cutter, built around a purchased frame. These frames can be found quite easily – try Google – and using one as a base for designing a bag or purse can make a good starting point.

1. The frame was laid on paper and a pattern for the front and back was drawn out. The front and back shapes were then cut out of Decovil – a non-woven fabric.

2. Using the rotary cutter, pieces were freely cut out of printed fabric and fusible film and bonded to the Decovil.

3. These were stitched down and the front and back pieces stitched together. The bag was then stitched onto the frame.

> A rotary cutter was used to cut shapes from printed fabric. They were then bonded to Decovil and stitched before the bag was fixed to a purchased frame.

< Cushion with centre panel made from heat-treated chiffon. Applied cut shapes, hand-stitched, were added. The edges use the buttonhole technique described here.

Buttonholes

Most sewing machines, even the old faithfuls, have buttonhole attachments and these can be used to great effect in edging techniques. For the cushion shown here, work like this:

1. Make buttonholes in a line on close-woven black cotton fabric.

2. Cut out the strip and fold in half along its length so that each buttonhole folds at the centre point.

3. Cut the buttonholes between the stitched lines.

4. Insert the strip into the cushion seam when making up.

5. Fold every other buttonhole into 'prairie points', with the edge of the point caught down with a stitch.

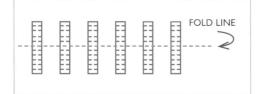

FOLD LINE

The buttonhole bag was worked in a similar way, with strips of buttonholes stitched on silk paper. The background silk was made by laying handfuls of silk fibre in opposing directions (much like making felt) and then soaking in a special solution. For more precise making instructions, see our free workshop at **www.d4daisy.com.**

It is a simple technique and the silk paper is very suitable as it doesn't fray. The bag shown on this page has buttonholes worked in metallic thread.

1. Cut out the shapes of the bag from silk paper first – you will need a back, front, base and sides.

2. Then apply strips of cut buttonholes to the front of the bag, building up from the bottom and stitching each row as you go along. The bag shown has these laid on the diagonal but that is open to experiment.

3. Edge the top with silk carrier rods, stitching them to the back of the bag opening and then allowing them to curl over the edge.

4. Finally, join all the seams and make a handle from more buttonhole strips.

∧ Bag made from strips of buttonholes stitched on a silk paper background. The bag was edged with carrier rods and the handle is another buttonhole strip.

Punches

These go by various names: punches, paper punches or craft paper punches. They vary from the simple hole punch or eyelet-maker to those that produce a range of shapes that fit together, or larger punches that can be aligned to make border patterns. You can see two of them here.

It is not always possible to tell when purchasing shaped punches whether they will cut anything other than paper. Obviously those that will cut fabric are a lot more useful and you may find that a firm non-woven fabric such as craft Vilene will cut well. However, even the paper option is useful as they are great for sketchbook work and can be combined with free-cut shapes to extend their range.

In the sketchbook below, the left-hand page shows painted book pages, cut with paper punches, and bonded to felt with added painted paper doilies. Right-hand page: positive and negative pieces were glued onto painted paper, torn into strips and woven together.

Interesting surfaces can be made by taking a background, perhaps painted card or fabric, and nibbling away at the edge with a punch – or possibly two punches. The cut-out shapes can be glued or stitched on top of the fabric, making a complex surface that is suitable for a variety of uses.

∧ Punched flowers and their negative shapes painted and glued to a background.

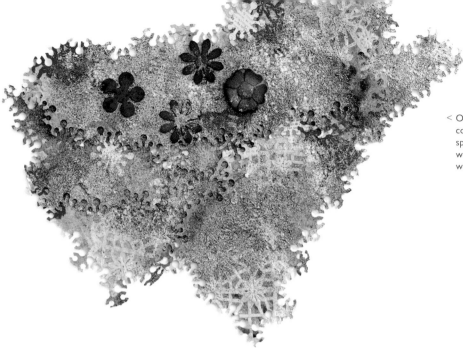

< Old book pages and doilies, painted and collaged onto card with embossing powder sprinkled on and heated while the glue is still wet. They were torn into strips and punches were used to cut patterns into the edges.

Working in strips

The disadvantage of the smaller punches is that you can only work around the edge. However, working on strips can extend their use. This way you can stamp in the centre and around the edges to produce a series of complex shapes. You can see an example of this in the wallhanging above.

This was made in the following way:

1. Paint and tear pages from unwanted books and glue them to a piece of background paper.

2. Paint some papers and paper doilies – bright colours are good.

3. Punch shapes from the paper and tear up the doilies.

4. Spread glue, quite thickly, over the background and scatter the shapes and doilies over the top.

5. Sprinkle embossing powder over the surface while the PVA is still wet and use a heat gun to melt the powder and make it bubble.

6. When dry, cut into strips and use a punch to make a decorative edge all around them.

7. Sew layers together using large hand stitches.

There are other advantages to strips. You might think about some of the following:

- weaving the strips
- leaving spaces between the strips to allow a background to show through
- using thin strips of felt to raise some strips before stitching them together.

If you can persuade your punch to cut shapes from craft Vilene, you have even more options to build up strips for vessels or book covers. Machine embroidery adds a further stitch option for all kinds of constructions.

Giving craft Vilene a light coat of gesso – the artist's foundation material found in art shops – makes painting easier. The pieces shown here have been painted with slightly watered-down acrylic paint after the gesso dried.

∧ Punched Vilene strips, coated with gesso and painted.

∨ A small book of pockets decorated with punched Vilene strips.

In order to see where the holes are cut when using a basic hole punch, work like this:

1. Mark the fabric with a small dot where the hole is needed.

2. Remove the loose base of the punch and, with the punch turned upside down, slide in the fabric and move it so that the dot is shown in one of the holes. Be careful that the other side of the punch is not making an unwanted hole.

3. Press down to cut out the hole and repeat to form holes in a random pattern over the strip.

∧ Single and combined motifs for three-dimensional flowers.

∧ Sample made from Vilene strips, coated with gesso and painted. These were raised with felt snippets under the strips to give height variation. This would be a good technique for a book cover.

∧ Two small punches designed to work together.

Combined punches

Some punches work together to make combined cut-outs which can be manipulated to form a three-dimensional shape – usually a flower. These can be fun when used to form garlands or tassels and are often tough enough to punch through fabric or craft Vilene. The flowers are joined by laying one over the other and then pulling the bottom petals through the top ones all the way around the shape. If you are ambitious, you can join three flowers this way.

Hole punches, eyelet tools and soldering irons

A hole punch can add to the potential of the decorated strips as holes can be formed between the motifs to enhance the effect. Even an office-type double-hole punch or a soldering iron will give a good result.

Eyelet tools are also useful and can often be purchased in sets, giving the option of different-sized holes. Soldering irons can be used in the same way by working on a heat-proof surface, making a single hole with the iron and then working around the edges of the hole to enlarge it. Take great care when using soldering irons in this way. Make sure they have a secure stand and never leave them unattended.

∨ Making holes with a soldering iron

Building up the surface

Surfaces can be built up using punched shapes with mixed media techniques. Here we are looking at using a base such as craft Vilene together with gesso. A surface built up on Vilene which has been coated with a thin layer of gesso can have punched shapes set into it or slightly protruding from the surface. This can then be painted and gilded. It is particularly suitable for three-dimensional pieces, such as the books shown here. Flat book covers would also be attractive made from this technique.

In addition to the gesso and Vilene, you will need some paints in a spray bottle and some salt. Gilding wax, such as Treasure Gold, can be useful, too.

Then work like this:

1. Cut three shapes from paper. Mine are usually faintly triangular, roughly 6 in (15 cm) high. Lay them over each other to make sure that they fit and then cut into the fronts if you are feeling creative.

2. When you are happy with the paper pieces, cut them from craft Vilene.

3. Punch some shapes from thin card. Cover the fronts with a layer of gesso, leaving the edges unpainted so that they can be stitched.

4. Set the punched shapes into the gesso surface. They can be partly submerged or set fairly well into the gesso. Some degree of protrusion makes it more interesting.

5. Spray as soon as you have finished, using a dark colour – it will fade a little due to the gesso. Allow to dry thoroughly. The inside should take some colour from the front and should not need painting.

6. Use a soldering iron or eyelet punch to make a pattern of holes in the surface. It will go through very easily but make sure you work on a heat-proof surface and take all the usual precautions with the soldering iron.

7. Using a coloured embroidery thread, buttonhole around the edges (these can be machined together but watch out for the gesso which will be quite hard).

8. When completely dry, try rubbing a little metallic wax lightly over the surface, using your finger to apply it. Pretend the surface is hot and you won't overdo it.

9. Make the inner pages from your favourite pretty paper, or stamp some handmade paper. I cut shapes from the inner pages using the same punch that was used for the card shapes. If your paper is very thin, give it a coat of acrylic wax which will add strength.

10. Place the pages together and make a hole near the top for a piece of braid or cord. Don't go too near the top in case the paper tears (another good reason for using acrylic wax). Use the cord to attach the pages to the cover.

For a variation of this idea, sprinkle a very small amount of salt into the surface at the end of step 4, while the gesso is wet and before painting. This will attract the paint and will give an interesting surface effect.

This technique can be used with the double-punch flowers. The flower shapes could be lightly coated with gesso before fixing them together. They could then be set into the Vilene/gesso fabric as described earlier, to achieve a more three-dimensional effect.

< Little tower books can be made using Vilene and gesso in a mixed media technique involving gesso and craft Vilene that shows the smaller punched motifs off to good effect.

SECTION 2
Creative die cutting

We have seen that, even on a simple scale, shape cutting has great potential. Even more exciting results can be obtained by using a die-cutting machine. Although the dies can cost about the same as some of the bigger punches, they are much better value. They are more detailed, do not blunt and can cut a variety of materials.

Buying one of the cutting machines won't break the bank – look out for special offers, or try eBay. There are often bargains to be found with basic hand machines as people move on to electronic wizardry. It's worth doing some research to find out what you need from the machine, so look online and check out your local craft centre where you can often try out the cutters. The basic machines can be used very creatively for stitching, quilting and mixed media work. They will cut and texture a wide range of materials, from paper to metal.

It is necessary to purchase dies (think of them as cookie cutters) for the machines and they can be expensive but we will show here that a large range of cutters is not necessary. During the making stage of this book we all became completely hooked on the shapes that remain after cutting, as you will see in subsequent sections.

Die-cutting machines have been around for some time. Even before the Industrial Revolution, it was recognised by some trades that hand cutting the same shape many times was tiresome – think of a cobbler cutting out shoe patterns. These days, of course, high-tech cutting machines are employed for everything from car parts to fashion cutting.

The use of die cutters is becoming much more popular with stitchers and mixed media fans as the choice and design of dies improve. The machines range from simple hand-operated types, through electric and onto computer-controlled equipment. Some have cartridges that give more options. You might think that cutting the same shapes over and over again would be boring – but we hope to convince you otherwise. Many of your favourite surface design and stitch techniques can be used, and the shapes will look different with each one – more on that later. In the meantime, let's consider the dies.

∨ Die-cutting machines. Shown here are the Sizzix Bigshot which will cut a large variety of materials. Also the Spellbinders Grand Calibur, which has a large cutting platform, and the Spellbinders Artisan Explorer. This is a high-pressure machine for cutting and embossing heavy metals and other materials for jewellery-making.

∧ A colourful range of cut shapes.

Dies

Dies vary with manufacturer and although there are many different forms, they all perform the same function of cutting into the material. Many of them work on all makes of die cutter but it is important to make sure that they are compatible with your machine by checking the labelling.

The usual method of cutting is to make a sandwich, with the material to cut and the die trapped between the cutting plates. Most machines have a range of options for getting the correct pressure, either by using chunky dies or padding with an arrangement of boards, known as platforms.

Some of the thicker dies are padded with foam so that the cutting element is buried. Others consist of just the cutter, and these are the ones that need the platform. Remember, when looking at the die, that there is usually a metal surround, so the die looks thicker than it is. Look on the packaging, where there is almost always an image showing how it will look when cut.

Follow the instructions for your machine and the die you are planning to use. If you are new to cutting, try paper first. You can make great shapes, simply cut from paper, for cards or sketchbook work. A small basic die can be used in many ways if it is combined with drawing, as the sketchbook on this page demonstrates.

In this section of the book we have listed the dies that we used, along with the main materials required for each technique. This doesn't mean that you have to have the same dies and it's much better to explore the ideas given using your own cut shapes.

∧ Sizzix machine in action, showing the platform, cutting plates and the Tattered Florals die.

> Sketchbook page created from Elegant Flourish die cuts and offcuts. After a coat of snow paint, these were arranged around a painted trunk to create a tree.

< Bracelet made from craft Vilene, painted and die-cut, then stitched together. The highlights were added with gold paint.

Basic cutting

Cutting shapes and applying them to a background is a good way to begin.

We found that a great all-purpose fabric to use for cutting is an interfacing such as craft Vilene. It is firm, doesn't fray and can be stitched easily. It is a bit greedy with runny paints, such as silk paints, but works very well with other paint techniques. You might consider trying the following:

- Add a little water to acrylic paint to make it easier to spread.
- Experiment with transfer paints and dyes – the ones where you paint on paper and iron across onto fabric.
- Work with gesso (used for preparing a canvas for painting) sprayed with ink or spray paints.
- Acrylic or metallic wax as a final coat will give a lovely effect.

Any of these colouring methods can be significantly enhanced with the application of a Derwent Coloursoft pencil or two – any easy-blend pencil or crayon will work but the Coloursoft are the best we've found. They are very soft and ideal for blending – a blending tool can help here. They also work well on top of liming wax – a product used to achieve a distressed look on furniture.

We will cover most of these methods later in the book but here is one to start you off. The bracelet above was made from a craft Vilene background and combined two dies, cut from thinner Vilene. Small flower shapes and leaves (cut using the Sizzix Garden Greens leaf-shaped die) were painted with acrylic paint and then stitched to painted Vilene. A little gold paint or metallic wax gave a gilded effect when all was dry.

Be aware of the negative shapes that remain when you have cut out all your pieces. These can often make great borders, or even complete artworks. When working on a piece with multiple cut-outs, consider preparing the material to be cut as a long strip. If it doesn't work with the current piece, tuck it away for later use. There is more on this in Section 4.

The books shown here were cut from computer-printed Lutradur and silk paper, supported by dyed felt. They were cut from Sizzix dies (Tim Holtz Arch Frame, and Sized Arches, Movers and Shapers), including the paper pages. Hand stitching stabilised the piece and gave it structure. When cutting the paper, allow for a fold within the edge of the dies to create a double spread.

∨ Two books made from silk paper pieces cut with the Arch Frame die and lined with dyed wool felt. The cover of the blue book used computer-printed Lutradur. The orange book was backed with orange glitter fabric which used the negative shapes from the Elegant Flourishes die. The inside pages were cut using the Movers and Shapers die.

Most fabrics cut well, and bonding fabrics with Heat'n'Bond (or a similar stabiliser) usually ensures that the edges won't fray. However, loose-weave material is best avoided. Close-weave materials, such as cotton, can be cut without bonding (if they are too fine, try spray starch, which washes out after use). Stiffen Stuff is a spray that also works well. Some sheers can be a problem, as they are too soft to cut well. They cut best if they are backed with Bondaweb fusible webbing or ironed onto freezer paper. A sheet of copier paper can also be placed on the cutting surface under the sheer fabric.

∧ The embossing folder can have ink added to the inside surface to print and emboss at the same time. This gives an attractive raised effect.

Embossing with a die cutter

In addition to the cutters, the machines can be used to impress a design in paper or metal without actually cutting through it. This is known as embossing and can really add to the range of possibilities. Many companies produce what are known as embossing folders.

These plastic folders can have cards inserted into the opening and the positive and negative sides of the design are impressed very deeply into the card when it is run through the machine.

This is really useful for making backgrounds. Embossing designs into painted and acrylic-waxed craft Vilene gives an embossed leather effect. If real leather is dampened, it will hold an embossed pattern well. Textured wrapping paper or wallpaper also work well. It is also an effective way to add pattern to metal, acetate, cardboard or painted felt and especially good for making embellishments by adding pattern to die-cut shapes.

Inkpads can be used on the positive side of the inside surface of the folder to print colours on the card as it is being embossed.

∨ Book pages made from two pieces of crumpled, painted brown paper, bonded with Heat'n'Bond. Some pages were embossed with patterns. This one includes torn, painted, textured wrapping paper. The copper butterfly was die-cut and patterned with a spent ballpoint pen.

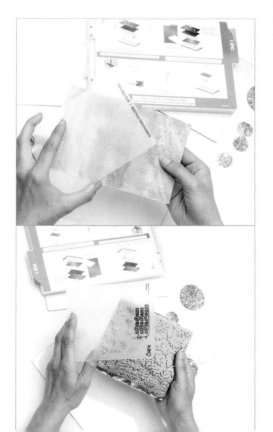

Beyond the basics

It is possible to cut shapes from a wide range of materials. Paper, card and fabric are the first things that come to mind, but metal and stitched surfaces can work really well too. Heat-tool techniques can also be used to add excitement.

Think about your favourite techniques or consider some of the following:
- texture paints on fabric
- machine-couched threads on felt or craft Vilene
- applied fabrics or silk rods on felt
- built-up layered surfaces bonded together
- zapped heat-reactive felt, painted with metallic paints
- machine stitching on water-soluble film or fabric.

Let's examine some of these ideas in more depth.

Heat-reactive felt and embossing powder

As the die-cutting machines are now used for much more than just paper crafts, some companies have started to produce dies specifically for cutting shapes for quilters. These can be used to cut traditional shapes from more unusual materials to make quilt-inspired mixed-media pieces, such as the box, shown opposite.

1. Make a base fabric by applying paint to a base of heat-reactive Kunin felt. Leave some areas almost free of paint.

2. Before the paint dries, sprinkle with embossing powder and then shake off the excess.

3. Use a heat tool to activate the embossing powder and, while still liquid, push a stamp into it. Take great care not to touch the hot powder.

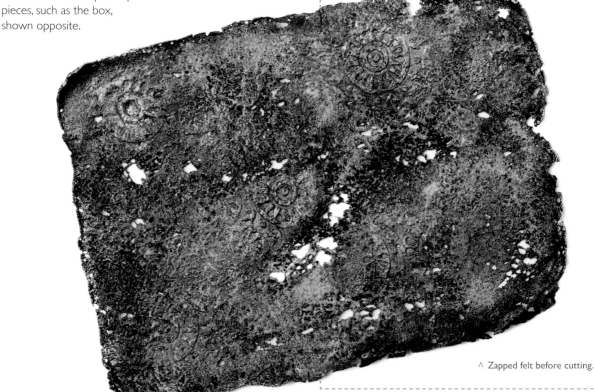

∧ Zapped felt before cutting.

< Box made from
watercolour paper
and embellished with
hexagons cut from
the zapped felt and
craft Vilene.

This could be taken to another level by painting Kunin felt and craft Vilene with PVA glue and then dipping them in a variety of different-coloured embossing powders.

The shapes shown here were repeatedly heated, glued and heated again to give a deep build-up of colour and texture to resemble enamel. The heating also melted the surface of the felt to give an eroded effect.

The hexagons were cut in two sizes from the felt and Vilene using Sizzix quilting dies and were combined with hand stitching to make a box.

The box base was made by painting heavy watercolour paper with acrylic and metallic paints. This was cut into a box shape using a template. The sides were stitched using silk thread. Hexagons were made from the distressed felt described above, from craft Vilene and watercolour paper, layered and glued on. More hexagons, cut from shrink plastic and shrunk, were attached to a copper chain to make a dangly embellishment for the lid.

< Tassel made from silk carrier rods, ironed flat and stitched onto felt. Leaf shapes were then cut out and formed into the head of a tassel.

Carrier rod tassels

YOU WILL NEED:

- Dies: Sizzix Tim Holtz Tattered Leaves, Crafts-Too, Small Floral CTD17069
- Felt
- Couched yarns/silk carrier rods/snippets of fabric
- Heavyweight silk or rayon yarn

⌐ Small leafy dies make great embellishments for tassels. They tend to curl well when cut from craft Vilene, painted and edged with buttonhole stitch.

> Silk carrier rods.

This method works with couched yarns, silk carrier rods or snippets of fabric, all of which have been stitched onto felt. The felt is good because it won't fray. Take care with the material you are placing on top and stick to closely woven or non-woven fabric. Silk rods are a waste product from silk spinning and they can be peeled apart or used just as they are.

1. Iron the rods to make them flat.

2. Stitch them onto felt – a dark colour works best and a straight stitch or machine pattern can be used.

3. Cut out the shapes with a large, not too fussy, die. You will need six to eight pieces. Hand stitching could be added, if you wish.

4. Cut a piece of felt as a base – a good size to start with would be about 8 x 8 cm (about 3 x 3 in). Fold it in three to give a fat strip. The skirt of the tassel will go through this strip and the felt will make a firm base to build up your cut-outs for the tassel head.

5. Wind a heavyweight silk or rayon yarn around a suitable-sized piece of card to make the skirt. Cut it off the card and lay it on the felt strip with the centre of the silk in the centre of the felt.

6. Pull up the side of the felt to make a loop and tie the skirt just under the loop.

7. Stitch the felt together at the top – hand stitch is usually easiest.

8. Now pin your cut-out shapes around the felt until you are happy with the arrangement. Then stitch them securely to the felt, or to each other.

9. Smaller shapes, cut from craft Vilene and painted, can be used as 'danglies'. They look really lovely if you buttonhole the edges with metallic thread.

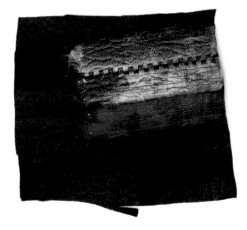

Symmetry

Although at first glance the cutters only cut one way, do remember that you can reverse a cut shape on any fabric that has no 'right side' just by turning the fabric over. Craft Vilene is a very useful material for this reason and it also cuts very cleanly. For right-sided fabrics follow the steps bellow.

YOU WILL NEED:

- Die: Spellbinders In-spire (In Flight)
- Felt
- Bondaweb fusible webbing
- Silk
- Silk paints
- Hand-stitching threads
- Yarn for tassel skirt

For fabric with a right side, just place your material upside-down on the cutter. For instance, the bird shapes shown here are cut from silk bonded to felt. The die used is in the form of a bird but, when manipulated into a symmetrical shape, it has turned into a flower. Any die that is not too small and fiddly will work for this technique. For the tassel shown, work like this:

1. Cut a strip of white felt, white silk and Bondaweb to the same size and then bond the silk to the felt.

2. Cut a strip from the fabric that fits the cutter, and lay the die on the strip with the fabric right side up and cut.

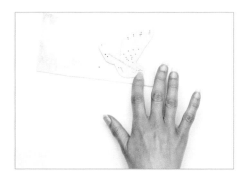

3. Cut another bird like this, and then two more with the fabric wrong side up. This should give you four symmetrical shapes.

4. Dampen the shapes and paint with silk paints, scattering some salt if you like that effect. Allow to dry.

5. Hand or machine stitch around the edge of the shape to give it greater definition. I find a buttonhole stitch is ideal.

6. Place two of the smaller shapes together and pin from the back. Pin the other two together and see how they work as a symmetrical shape. Keep experimenting until you are happy with the tassel head. Be careful to pin only through the felt as the pins will mark fine silk. When you like the effect, stitch three shapes together, leaving an opening for the skirt.

7. Make a tassel skirt by winding a heavyweight silk or rayon yarn around a suitably sized piece of card to make the skirt. Cut it off the card and tie it firmly at the centre point. (You could bead the tassel top at this point.) Attach the skirt using a toning silk thread and trim to obtain the length required.

∧ A bird-shaped die was cut from fine silk, bonded to felt. This was cut from both the right side and the wrong side of the fabric in order to achieve a symmetrical shape. The result was hand-stitched and formed into a tassel.

Trapping cut shapes

Cut-out shapes can be trapped in layers of silk paper for an intriguing surface. If you have never made silk paper, go to **www.d4daisy.com** and follow the tutorial.

Cut shapes with silk paper

YOU WILL NEED:

- Dies: Sizzix Snowflakes, Sizzix Tattered Leaves
- Silk paper
- Silk fibres and CMC paste

> This silk paper bowl with trapped silk paper leaves was machine-stitched while flat. The piece was wet with CMC glue and moulded around a bowl to create its shape.

> Silk paper piece using trapped thick felt Snowflake die cuts. The piece was machine and hand-stitched.

Here is how to make the bowl shown opposite.

1. Create two pieces of silk paper, one for your bowl and the other for the shapes you want to cut out. The paper to be die-cut can be thicker and in a contrasting colour for greater visibility.

2. For a bowl, aim to create a circular piece – but there's no need to be too precise … a bit of irregularity will suit the shape. Allow both pieces to dry.

3. Cut your silk paper into shapes or die-cut shapes.

4. Arrange the shapes on the piece of circular silk paper.

5. Cover with a thin layer of fibres to trap the shapes – enough to trap them but not so much that they are obscured.

6. Re-apply the silk fibres and CMC paste to the whole piece. Leave to dry.

7. Machine or hand stitch and embellish as you wish. It is easier to do this on a flat piece.

8. Reapply more CMC paste and drape the silk paper over a bowl. Place the bowl over a jar or tin to raise it up if required.

9. For flat pieces, the base layer, cut shapes and top layer can all be worked at the same time and embellishments added when dry.

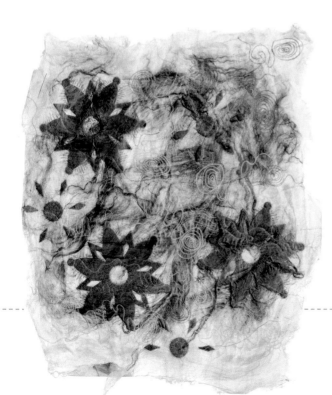

Combining die cuts with stencils and stamps

YOU WILL NEED:

- Dies: Sizzix Elegant Flourishes, Sizzix Sizzlets Bird, Swallow
- Stencil Girl Sparrow stencil
- Dark cotton fabric
- Crystal spun-bonded fabric
- Thermofax screen
- Lutradur
- Fusible film
- Bondaweb fusible webbing
- Snow paint
- Xpandaprint

Using die cuts alone can be limiting, especially if you don't have many dies. Combining them with other dies and stencils, both commercial and handmade, can open up opportunities and really let your imagination fly.

This cape is a good example of taking a small number of components and bringing them together to create a complex surface that is deceptively simple to produce. A cape requires only a straightforward pattern. Start with a giant circle template cut out of paper. You can try it on and alter the shape to make it what you want. Here, the front and back measurements were shortened to create an oval shape and the front was cut away to make an opening.

When the pattern had been completed, two pieces were cut out from a dark cotton backing fabric and a piece of crystal spun-bonded fabric. Using the crystal spun-bonded fabric, gesso was applied through the Sparrow stencil, working in a random way over the entire surface to create a pattern, concentrating the heavier application along the base of the cape and up the centre back for symmetry.

A phrase of text pushed through a custom-made Thermofax screen provided further embellishment. At this point the spun-bonded fabric was pinned on top of the cotton and they were then treated as one fabric.

Moving on to die cuts, only two dies were used:
- Flourishes were cut from Lutradur which had been fabric-painted and printed using blue fabric paints and gesso.
- Swallows were cut from fusible film (backed carefully with Bondaweb prior to cutting).

Angelina fibres and Bondaweb (with silver transfoil) were applied. The white birds 'flying' around the base were stencilled onto Lutradur with snow paint and Xpandaprint and then the surrounding Lutradur was zapped away with a heat tool. These shapes were stitched to the base before the entire piece was machine stitched, both for decoration and to anchor the die cuts. The cape was assembled with lining fabric and a collar to finish.

> Cape created using commercial fabric and crystal spun-bonded fabric, which was stencilled with a commercial stencil and embellished with die cuts from Elegant Flourishes and Swallow dies. Larger birds were arranged around the cape using the Sparrows stencil with Xpandaprint and snow paint.

Plastic and metal

Moving even further from the basics, some of the most unlikely materials work wonderfully well with the die cutters. Metal shim and the special plastic that reacts to heat by shrinking are real stars in this respect.

∧ Inkjet-printed shrink plastic makes great buttons.

Shrink plastic

This plastic can be coloured in many ways – it could be painted with acrylic paints, sprayed with metallic or decorated with embossing powder after cutting. There is also the option of rubbing down the smooth surface and crayoning it. There is even a type available for inkjet-printing. It can then be cut and heat applied to make it smaller and so intensify the colour. It has some intriguing possibilities for cutting. Take care to cut out pieces along the same orientation as the material sometimes shrinks more in one direction.

The Sizzix Elisse die has two sizes of arch tag on one die. This shrink plastic book has the smaller arch fused to the larger arch on the front. The shrink plastic fuses to itself when hot, so just place the heated smaller shape over the larger one, being careful not to burn your fingers. Then press down with a block or something similar.

∧ Printed and painted shrink plastic, cut with a hexagon die. Holes were made so that they could be used as jewellery or attached to fabric.

< This shrink plastic book was made from painted shrink plastic cut using a die designed for tags. It is shown next to a concertina book made from the same die to show the extent of the shrinkage.

Shrink plastic book

YOU WILL NEED:

- Die: Sizzix Elisse
- Shrink plastic
- Lumiere paint
- Hole punch
- Heat-treated copper
- Embossing folders
- Jewellery jump rings

To create the tiny book, you will need an A5 piece of shrink plastic.

1. Sand it vertically and horizontally and stipple the front with three colours of Lumiere paint. Aim to get lots of texture. Leave to dry. Paint the back with a different colour if you wish.

2. Cut it in half and die-cut each piece with the Sizzix die Elisse.

3. With insides together, punch two holes on one side for the binding.

4. Use a heat tool to shrink the plastic. The paint will bubble as it shrinks, giving a lot of texture and intensifying the colours. As soon as it has shrunk, flatten it with the back of a wooden stamp.

5. Cut a paper template for the pages and cut pieces of heat-treated copper to size.

6. Use the holes in the cover as a guide for piercing holes in the copper pages. Use embossing folders to texturise the pages with different patterns.

7. Bind together the covers and pages with jewellery jump rings.

> Cut pieces for the book and finished pieces after shrinking.

Metal

Metals can easily be cut on the die cutter. Even quite thick metal will cut easily. The basic rule is that anything that can be cut with scissors will be suitable in most die cutters. The fine metal shim that can be stitched with the sewing machine is also great because it can be stitched afterwards. Metal can be given a texture by drawing into it with an embossing tool or old ballpoint pen and, of course, it is a natural for the embossing folders that go through the die cutters. The bracelet shown here has been textured in this way.

Bracelet

Cutting the metal for this piece of work resulted in some interesting shapes remaining after the circles were cut. You can see what happened to them in Section 4, page 67. To make the bracelet, follow these instructions.

> Embossed and painted craft Vilene bracelet decorated with die-cut copper circles.

YOU WILL NEED:

- – Die: Circular die in a suitable size
- – Metal circles cut using the die
- – Craft Concept Tuscan Tiles embossing folder
- – Craft Vilene
- – Acrylic wax
- – Brad pins and jewellery findings
- – Hole punch
- – Tim Holtz Hitch Fastener

1. Paint craft Vilene and give it a coat of acrylic wax when the paint is dry.

2. Measure and shape a piece of this fabric to make a bracelet and add texture by running it through the Craft Concept Tuscan Tiles embossing folder.

3. Decorate the metal for the circles, emboss and cut.

4. Attach them to the Vilene with brad pins and jewellery findings. Make a hole with a darning needle and push the brad or finding through it.

5. Make a closure by punching a hole in both ends and attach a Tim Holtz Hitch Fastener through one of the holes.

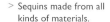
> Sequins made from all
  kinds of materials.

v Clear acetate book
  cover with attached
  sequins made from
  embossed, alcohol-inked
  metal and acetate.

Sequins and buttons

Really effective decorative effects can be
achieved when you make custom-built sequins.
This is a great way of using up small pieces of
metal left over from other cuts, or even waste
acetate from packaging. Simply colour the metal
with acrylic paint or alcohol inks and then die-cut
circles from the metal in different sizes. These
could be textured using a variety of embossing
folders. They can then be pierced through the
middle with a darning needle.

The sequins can be made in all sizes, and circle
hand punches are great for them. You could also
consider using painted acetate or shrink plastic
for sequins. If using shrink plastic, one of the
larger circular dies might be best – remember
how much they shrink. Shrink plastic circles make
great washable buttons.

< Sketchbook page created using circles cut from black foam core board and Tissuetex, decorated with commercial stencils and die-cut circle waste.

∨ Wallhanging created using roundels cut from metal, Tissuetex and hand-printed fabric. The metal was embossed and coloured with alcohol inks. Stencils were used to create an interesting edge. The piece was machine-stitched once the roundels were in place.

Take one shape

Sam and Paula have used circular dies of various sizes to show how many looks can be achieved with just one shape. Many of the companies sell sets of circles in different sizes. Even the negative of the cut-outs looks exciting when placed on a colourful background together with some circles, and gives ideas for the layering and stitching that can combine in a completed piece of work.

The colours of this impromptu sample inspired Sam's machine-embroidered hanging, with roundels of various sizes contrasting on a fabric-painted background. The die was also used to cut into the edge of the fabric, giving a coherent feeling to the piece. It was sympathetically textured with free machine embroidery which enhanced the shape of the circles and gave movement. The addition of circles cut from metal shim gave a stunning metallic gleam.

Negative shapes

Paula used the negative shapes from the Spellbinders circle die set to make a delightful concertina book. These sets include shapes ranging from 1 cm upwards and the dies can be placed individually anywhere on a surface to make your own combinations of pattern.

A long piece of craft Vilene was used for the book and the dies placed all along the surface. The cutting was considered very carefully, not only using the circles to provide a change of scale, but also to make the view through the book as interesting as possible. A soldering iron gave even smaller circles.

After cutting, the craft Vilene was transfer painted and the colours were enhanced with Derwent Coloursoft pencils which blend really well on the Vilene. It was then coated with acrylic wax. Various hand stitches were worked around the holes and in the areas between them.

∧ A craft Vilene concertina book with circles cut with Spellbinders dies to give a view through the book. It has been coloured with Derwent Coloursoft pencils, acrylic waxed and decorated with a soldering iron and hand stitch.

∨ The book after stitching.

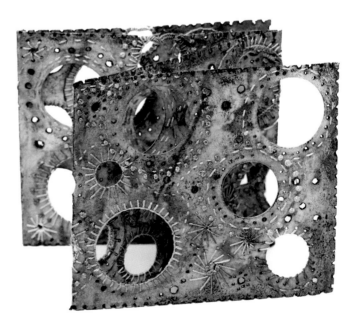

Water-soluble materials

It is very difficult to sew patterns, particularly circular ones, with freehand stitching. Using die-cut circles or other tricky shapes, you can achieve more accurate designs. Just use the die to cut out your shapes from sticky water-soluble fabric, such as Aquabond, and stick them onto your surface. Then lay more circles on top of one other to assist with sewing circles within circles. Follow the shape of the water-soluble fabric to stitch; then wash away the water-soluble fabric.

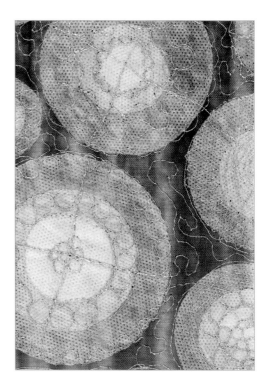

∧ Self-adhesive water-soluble fabric circles were used as a stitching guide on hand-dyed fabric – seen here before dissolving.

< The water-soluble fabric was then dissolved to leave perfect circles.

Water-soluble with cut shapes

Water-soluble fabrics can be cut out before the base fabric is dissolved. This technique also provides the option of joining stitched motifs or building up lacy surfaces.

YOU WILL NEED:

- Dies: Sizzix Artful Dwellings, Asymmetrical Rings
- Lacy trim
- Aquabond sticky water-soluble fabric
- Water-soluble film

The top collar was made from lacy trim which had been cut out using the Artful Dwellings die. This lace was firm enough to cut without stiffening, but if you are using fine lace try a stiffener or spray starch before cutting. The connecting pieces were made from the tips of the same die shape combined with a circle die to create a curved base.

These cut shapes were applied to Aquabond, a sticky water-soluble fabric. They were arranged in a collar shape. A piece of water-soluble film was placed over the top and then the collar band was created by heavy machine embroidery, connecting all the pieces by stitch. The water-soluble fabric was then washed away.

The lower collar was made from hand-dyed cotton circles cut from Asymmetrical Rings also applied to sticky water-soluble fabric. A strip of fabric to make the collar band was cut and placed on the surface. It was machine stitched to trap all the circles and the collar band.

> The orange collar was created from the Asymmetrical Rings die and cut from hand-dyed fabric which was adhered to self-adhesive water-soluble fabric. The collar was heavily machine-stitched to link the circles into a collar shape.

The black and white collar shown above it was formed from a lacy trim, cut from the Artful Dwellings die and stitched together using self-adhesive water-soluble fabric.

Lettering

A lettering die can be an extremely useful addition to your die library. Nothing customises your work in the way that a message does. Text can be random or formal. It can explain, tease, embellish or just be a decorative element in its own right.

Lettering as decoration

In this text piece, various techniques were used. A quotation from *The Tempest* (Caliban's soliloquy) was chosen, using the Wordplay and Sans Serif dies. The base fabric was cotton, painted with a weak walnut ink wash. Two main techniques were used:

1. **Die cuts as stencils:** using the Wordplay die, the alphabet was cut out of freezer paper several times. The negative shapes were cut up and ironed onto the fabric in a random manner and stencilled with Stewart Gill Chestnut paint.

2. **Die cuts as masks:** the freezer-paper letters from the previous step were ironed on randomly and then gesso was sponged on the surface.

∧ The Sizzix Wordplay die was used on heavyweight Vilene. Although this cuts right through the material, the letters are not easily dislodged and will remain in situ. Card or duct tape can then be fixed over the back to hold them in place and give an interesting background. It is even better with lettering placed on top.

YOU WILL NEED:

- Dies: Sizzix Wordplay and Sans Serif
- Cotton fabric
- Walnut ink wash
- Stewart Gill Chestnut paint
- Freezer paper
- Aquabond adhesive water-soluble fabric
- Water-soluble fabric
- Craft Vilene
- Soldering iron
- Script stamp
- Crystal spun-bonded fabric
- Rotary cutter
- Foam

1. Fabrics of graduated colour were die-cut and bonded onto the surface in a random fashion.

2. Adhesive water-soluble fabric was used to guide stitching. Letters, cut out of water-soluble fabric, were stitched directly onto the surface of the piece. As the stitching was dense, the water-soluble fabric was not washed away.

3. Cut shapes were bonded to craft Vilene. An outline of each letter was stitched and then cut out with a soldering iron. The letters were hand-stitched onto the piece.

4. To create an edging, fabric was bonded to wadding. Letters were then cut out using the Sans Serif die. These were stamped with a script stamp and placed so that the letters protruded from the edge of the piece. Further stitch was completed around the letters.

< A random font was used in layers to build up a background, after which a quotation from *The Tempest* was stitched separately and placed on top. The wallhanging uses freezer-paper stencils and masks, self-adhesive water-soluble text and craft Vilene lettering. These were all die-cut from the Wordplay and Sans Serif Sizzix dies.

Lettering for a message

This large three-piece panel is all about pretty things hiding nasties. You can, I'm sure, think of your own application whether political, related to your work environment or even a 'snake in the grass' friend.

YOU WILL NEED:

- Dies: Tattered Leaves and Tattered Florals by Tim Holtz for Sizzix
- Gesso
- Craft Vilene
- Salt
- Quink ink
- Blue spray paint
- Golden Fluid Acrylic in Stainless Steel

The gesso, salt and paint technique from page 10 in Section 1 of this book gave an idea for the technique and colour scheme for this piece but it was constructed on a much larger scale. The background and dies were cut from craft Vilene.

Leaves and flowers were cut and set into the background with a light coating of gesso. Both the positive and negative of the cut leaf shapes were also used, as follows:

1. Three long rectangles were cut from the Vilene and coated very lightly with gesso.

2. The Vilene leaf shape was laid on the background in places and gesso was applied over the top with a palette knife.

3. The leaf was then lifted off very carefully to reveal the Vilene below.

4. In other places the negative of the cut shape was made into a stencil and gesso was applied through the shape.

5. The remainder of the background had more gesso applied with leaves and flowers set into it. The edge was partly covered with shapes or negatives of shapes. Likewise the letters of the word Metaphor.

6. Salt was sprinkled over the wet gesso and diluted Quink ink sprayed over the top. This gave a pale grey/blue colour which was accented in some areas by the application of a very light spray of blue water-based paint.

7. When the background was dry the large flowers were made. They were cut out twice for each bloom and wire was sandwiched between them to allow them to curve into shape.

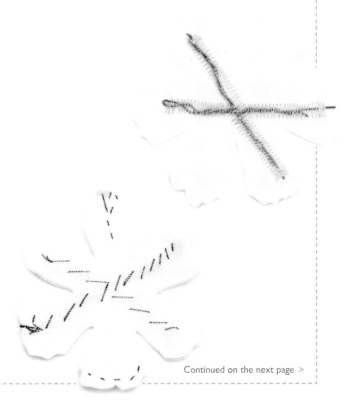

Continued on the next page >

< *Metaphor. 36 x 24 in (90 x 60 cm). These three pieces form a wallhanging that was inspired by the use of apparent good deeds to cover evil ones. It was made from craft Vilene, and gesso with applied leaves and wired flowers cut on the Sizzix machine.*

8. These large flowers were coated with gesso, inked and stitched to the background.

9. When all was dry, Golden Fluid Acrylic paint in the Stainless Steel colour was dry-brushed over the work. This makes a great glaze and is more subtle than wax.

10. The wire allowed the flower to curve into a three-dimensional shape.

11. A few beads were added to some of the flower centres.

12. The letters of the word Metaphor were cut from the Wordplay die and stuck to the background.

13. Finally, the lettering die was used to cut out a phrase – 'the evil that men do'. The letters were attached to a cord with beads.

∧ Detail showing how the lettering was made.

Multiple die-cutting

Dies are expensive, so it is worth considering whether it is possible to combine the dies in your collection to extend their use and make more interesting shapes. This is especially relevant when you are starting out and don't have many dies to play with. The purchase of a small, cheap die can extend your options considerably. The cutting can retain the general appearance of the larger die with one carefully considered cut, or you could do so much extra cutting that it becomes merely an abstraction of the original.

> Butterfly shapes with further die cuts.

When you have cut out your basic shapes, think about using other dies to cut into them. Smaller, delicate dies, such as scroll patterns, can work well here, but don't discount the idea of using the edge of a larger one. This method can add interest to large shapes and provide a more elegant conclusion. As an example we looked at a butterfly shape – a basic die which is excellent for this purpose as the wings are quite solid – offering lots of possibilities for using smaller, finer dies. Just cut out the initial shapes and then put them through the cutter again with the smaller die in position. Bear in mind the following points:

- The shape cut will be much finer than the die suggests, so try first on paper or card as this gives a good indication as to the placing of the die. This is not an exact science, so be prepared for unexpected results.
- As you cannot 'flip' the die, you won't get a perfectly symmetrical shape but the unexpected results of this second cut are all part of the fun. The shapes are linked and so have a harmony that satisfies.
- Don't be afraid to experiment – some combinations won't work but some will be magical.

These butterflies were stitched through the body on a painted silk ground. Their wings were allowed to remain unstitched and were bent upwards to give a three-dimensional effect.

< A butterfly die was used to cut the basic shape from craft Vilene. Further smaller dies were used to give more elegant shapes which were then mounted on silk-painted fabric.

> Three houses created using the Artful Dwellings die, cut from hand-dyed and printed fabric. The houses were stitched and embellished with beads and ribbons.

The third dimension

Unlike the 'free combining' of the previous section, some dies, such as Movers and Shapers, are designed to be used together. Others come in sizes that beg to be combined with larger dies. Here, Sam and Maggie are using the Artful Dwellings dies, which consist of four different building/structure shapes. Sam uses two Movers and Shapers dies, Mini Openings and Circles, to cut windows and doors, while Maggie uses a small scroll design with an Artful Dwellings shape to make triptych icons and shrines.

With Movers and Shapers, you can place the die exactly where you want it, either within a bigger die to cut in one go, or to create additional shape cuts within a previously cut piece.

Houses

All these houses were made from cotton fabric. The fabric doesn't need to be firm or non-fraying as the Soft and Stable stabiliser will strengthen it. All the edges were either satin-stitched or seam stitched.

Yellow house

Here, a Thermofax screen was used to transfer a design to the fabric. Choose one with fine lines or on a small scale. Waves by Thermofax Printing was used here. Add stitching if required.

1. Bond the fabric to Soft and Stable stabiliser. This sews and turns easily and is substantial enough to allow the house to stand.

2. Cut four identical pieces out of the largest house on the die. Cut windows if required, using the Openings die.

3. Stitch all the pieces right sides together along roof and wall edges.

4. Turn inside out and topstitch along the seams. This helps to shape the house.

5. Sew ribbon around the bottom edges. It helps to even out the base line.

Red and purple houses

1. Cut a piece of freezer paper using the Artful Dwellings die.

2. Cut out a design using a craft knife.

3. Cut out four pieces of fabric, bonded to Soft and Stable stabiliser.

4. Iron the freezer paper to each piece in turn and paint with fabric paints through the stencil.

5. Heat-set when dry.

6. Satin stitch around each piece to create a neat border.

7. With wrong sides together, stitch a straight stitch down each roof and edge just inside the satin stitch (red house) or hand stitch with right sides together (purple house).

8. If there is a gap at the top of the roof (it's sometimes tricky to fit each piece together exactly), use a large bead with stiff ribbons, threads or yarns cascading out of the top.

Metal icon

Another way of using this die is to work in metal. One of the larger shapes, together with two of the smaller ones, make a mock triptych.

Work like this:

1. Using a strong adhesive, stick craft Vilene to metal shim and leave overnight to set. Allow enough material to cut the shapes described above.

2. Cut into the shapes with a smaller die but don't cut too much away or it will weaken the metal. Save the cut-out shapes.

3. Use a sewing machine with no thread to create holes around the edges of the shape. A straight stitch, slightly longer than usual, works best (try some samples first on offcuts). These holes will allow you to stitch through the metal without having to worry about pushing a needle through it.

4. Straight stitch through the holes, using a silk or cotton embroidery thread. This is purely decorative stitching.

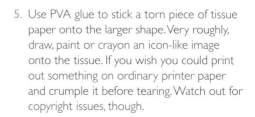

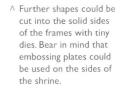

5. Use PVA glue to stick a torn piece of tissue paper onto the larger shape. Very roughly, draw, paint or crayon an icon-like image onto the tissue. If you wish you could print out something on ordinary printer paper and crumple it before tearing. Watch out for copyright issues, though.

6. Catch the three pieces together at the sides with a stitch or two to make mock hinges.

∧ Further shapes could be cut into the solid sides of the frames with tiny dies. Bear in mind that embossing plates could be used on the sides of the shrine.

The little 'shrine' houses are made in the same way except that four shapes are cut and the sewing machine holes are used to outline each of the four pieces with buttonhole stitch. A ladder stitch was used to join each piece. The cut-out allows a view through into the centre of the shrine. The tops remain unstitched. Embossing folders can be useful for adding texture.

∨ Shrines and icons were made from metal shim and the Artful Dwellings die.

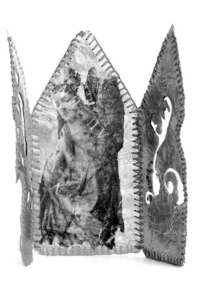

Printing collagraphs with a die cutter

Collagraphs are made by gluing components such as textured paper, lace, scrim or cut shapes to a piece of firm card or mountboard. In this example we are experimenting with textures but die-cut shapes, combined with free-hand cutting, also work very well. In an ideal world, you can't beat a proper press for printing the collagraph plates but you will find that a die-cutting machine, such as the Sizzix, will provide enough pressure to make a very acceptable substitute. There are many sites online that show how to make the plates so we will give brief instructions and then concentrate on the printing.

Making the plate

1. Cut a rectangle or square of mountboard to make a base. This must be narrower than the width of the die cutter.

2. Arrange elements on the card. These could be fragments of texture such as scrim or Kozo fibres, textured wallpaper or small pieces of lace. Alternatively, you could cut a design from thin card using either freehand cutting or die-cut shapes.

3. Arrange these on the card background and stick down firmly using PVA glue.

4. When dry, waterproof the whole plate by painting at least two coats of Shellac on the front, sides and back.

When it is dry, the plate can be used many times to make beautiful textured prints.

∧ Collagraph plate made as an experiment with textures.

Printing

1. Before you start printing, cut your paper to size. Allow enough paper for a small border around the print but, again, make sure it is slightly narrower than the width of the machine.

2. Leave the paper to soak in a container of water for at least ten minutes and then place it between two sheets of blotting paper to remove the excess water. It should be damp, not wet.

3. Before you print with paint, you can make an embossed or blind print by running the plate and a piece of paper through the machine. The thickness of the card used for the plate will determine how you use the cutting platform. For this mountboard plate we removed one of the leaves from the platform and built it up with felt. Cut a few pieces of felt or wool, slightly narrower than the width of the machine and slightly longer than your longest plate.

4. Place the plastic cutting plate on the platform, then the collagraph plate, textured side up. The slightly damp paper goes on top, followed by the other cutting plate. Now build up rectangles of felt (we used three) on top. The cutting plates are not involved in any cutting but will protect your machine from paint as they are easily wiped after printing.

5. Roll this sandwich through the machine. If it is too hard to roll through, take away a layer of the platform or a piece of felt. Check that it has embossed correctly. If the pressure has been insufficient to emboss the paper, add another layer of felt.

6. Now to add ink or paint. Squeeze out some acrylic printing ink or acrylic paint onto a piece of plastic or glass. The acrylic paint could be mixed with Daler-Rowney acrylic printing medium to a fairly runny consistency. Tear small pieces of mountboard to spread the paint onto the plate and use a brush to work it into the grooves and textured areas.

7. Use a wad of muslin or a paper towel to wipe the ink from the surface of the plate. This seems wasteful but it is essential. Then prepare as in step 4.

8. Feed the sandwich through, as before. Peel off the print and allow to dry. Make sure that you clean all the equipment thoroughly afterwards.

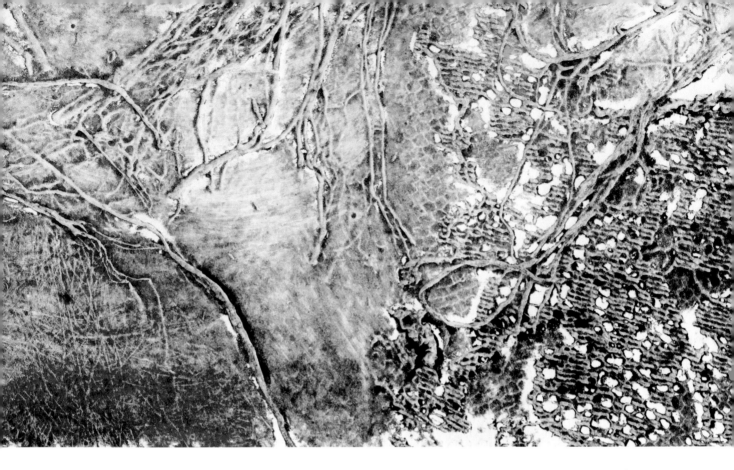

∧ Result of printing from the
  texture plate shown on page 41.

∨ Circular collagraph plate and print which
  were made up of a combination of free-cut
  shapes, lace and fragments of die-cut card.

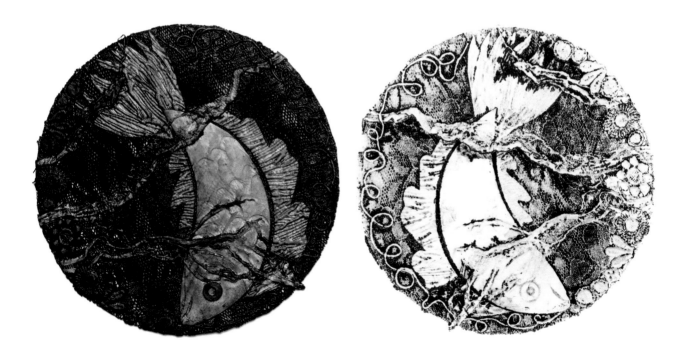

SECTION 3
Digital cutting

We hope we've inspired you in the earlier sections of the book with lots of ideas for using die-cutting machines, and also in how to consider methods of manipulation and disguise to enable you to get the maximum use from a limited number of dies. There's no getting away from the fact that, when cutting, the freedom to use your own drawings and designs offers limitless possibilities. It has long been feasible to have your own designs laser cut and the results are excellent, as you can see from Kim Thittichai's jewellery on this page. However, this can be an expensive option – fine if it is just used for a few, one-off pieces but not for everyday use.

However, there are increasingly good home-based solutions. A number of machines on the market can make this dream come true and some are surprisingly affordable. In general, they work in the following ways:

- Cutters that link to your PC and have their own software so that you can download scanned designs and operate free of the internet.
- Cutters that link to an online source through your PC. These are dependent on a good internet connection, as the software is all held online and your scanned design must be uploaded to the site to be converted into a suitable file format for the cutter to read.
- Stand-alone scanner cutters, such as the Brother Scan N Cut. These have a built-in scanner for your designs, which can then be manipulated and cut. This machine does not need to be connected to the internet or to a computer.

There is also a cut-work option for Bernina machines that have an embroidery unit but that lies beyond the scope of this book.

We are very grateful to Brother for the loan of a Scan N Cut machine. Most of our work in this section is based on this machine, but could be adapted to any of the computer-controlled cutters.

∨ Kim Thittichai makes colourful jewellery by sending her designs to a specialist laser cutter. They are then cut from heavyweight Vilene, with an application of foiled 'glitz'.

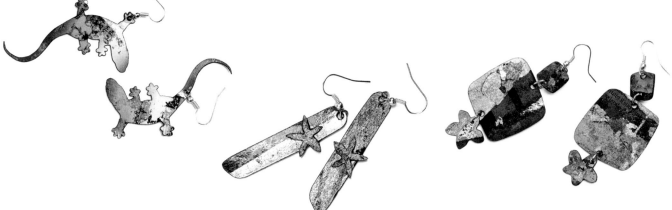

∧ The Brother Scan N Cut machine is wonderfully versatile. It scans your own design and also has a good variety of built-in shapes.

Some machines also include the option of using pens to add colour to your designs, which can be especially good for cards. We haven't included those in this book as we are really hooked on the cutting elements. Most of the digital machines have designs that are built-in or available on cartridges. They usually have good lettering facilities and lots of options to customise shapes. There are almost always further designs for cutting that can be purchased and downloaded.

Not all the machines cut fabric as well as the hand-operated die cutters, although most of them give good results with paper, card, metal and all forms of Vilene. Some will cut wood veneers quite happily. Commercial felt often cuts well but handmade felt can be tricky. Starching fabrics, especially finer ones, can be the best way to produce good results.

As with any new piece of equipment, it is worth taking time to sit down and play with all the basics, perhaps using one of the built-in designs, in order to become acquainted with how your machine works. This is hard when you are desperate to get on and create with your own drawing, but it will be worth it and will save you time in the long run.

> Butterfly dangly. This was cut using an electronic cutter for the butterflies. They were threaded with beads and shells to make a mobile for a conservatory.

Built-in designs

Most of the digital systems include a good selection of shapes. One of the big advantages with all of them is the control that you have over the shape, size and orientation of the motifs. By stretching the width and length, you can alter the shape of a built-in design, often producing something very unusual that is nothing like the original. Changing the scale is also interesting and an obvious early step to try. Even changing the placement of the motif allows for greater creativity as they can be manipulated in so many ways, allowing them to cut into each other, giving yet another shape. Don't forget to try combining a couple of motifs, particularly with an eye to the negative shapes that will be produced when they are cut.

The layout screen is your best friend and, because the cut is so clean, you'll find that the area remaining after the cut will often form a stencil that will become part of the work. It is also possible to link built-in shapes with text, as you can see on the opposite page.

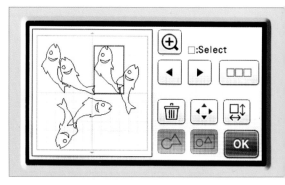

This fish design is one of the zodiac signs included in the Brother Scan N Cut machine. If it is cut creatively with some of the shapes overlapping, it gives a more interesting selection of units to play with. Most of the machines show the layout screen clearly and manipulating the shapes is very simple.

These shapes were cut from craft Vilene and went on to become a vessel – in every sense of the word. The overlapped fishes were machined together to make the most of their unusual shapes.

> Cut-outs of fishes, painted and machine stitched. Some were over-cut to vary the shape.

∨ Fishy boat. Fish shapes were painted, coloured with spray paint and Coloursoft pencils, and then stitched, tail up, into a bowl shape. Three fishes, which were cut more creatively, were machine embroidered and placed in their 'vessel'.

∨ Inbuilt leaf and text designs were arranged and merged together to create a wreath and text. You can see the design on the screen and a detail of the cutting (right).

∧ Lynda Monk's work was cut using a Cameo Silhouette cutting machine. The piece shows an interesting use of lettering.

Lettering

Lettering offers so many options and, again, is a good starting point for mastering the software. It is a great joy to be able to select the letters that you want so easily, rather than the somewhat fiddly procedure for isolating individual letters on the hand machines.

There is usually a good choice of fonts built into the machine or the software and you can type out anything from single letters to a series of words. It is possible to mix text within your design but, as most of the machines deal with this as a different element, you may have to use the 'unify' or 'group' command to keep it all together.

Stencils work well with text and are especially useful with the Gelli Plate. Try using Deli Paper for this. It is a cross between tissue paper and baking paper which is thin, strong and can be used for printing. It doesn't disintegrate in the same way as tissue paper does when wet.

It is also good to work in lettering for sketchbooks where the page underneath will show through. A phrase could be typed up individually and the layout screen used for accurate placement on the page. Most systems allow for precise size adjustment to fit the surface that you are going to cut.

∧ Sketchbook page created from watercolour paper. It was stencilled with shapes and text cut from Deli Paper using the Brother Scan N Cut machine.

< Sketchbook pages using lettering from an inbuilt design, arranged to fit onto each page and cut out on the Scan N Cut machine. They were painted afterwards with Dyelusions Spray Inks and Koh-i-noor dye paints.

< Tabbed pages of watercolour paper created for a sketchbook. Each tab was created on the Scan N Cut from a drawn house shape and inlaid with a letter. The letters were all cut on the Scan N Cut.

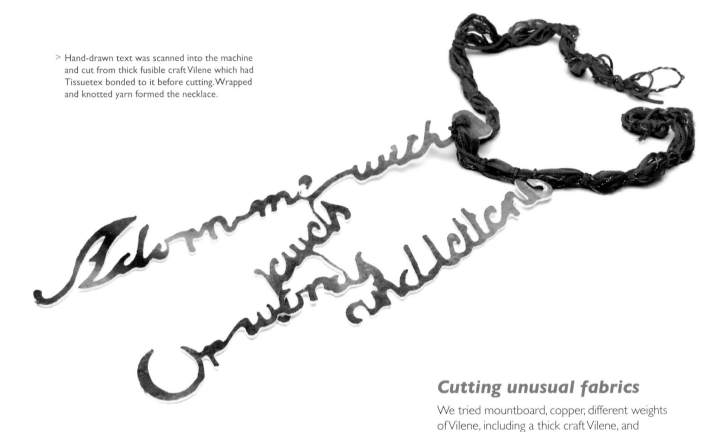

> Hand-drawn text was scanned into the machine and cut from thick fusible craft Vilene which had Tissuetex bonded to it before cutting. Wrapped and knotted yarn formed the necklace.

Using your own text

You can write your own text and scan it in to cut out. If you need it to be cut out in a continuous piece, you must ensure that the design is made using one line that hasn't left the paper. The text might not be as clear, but it is a great effect. Cutting the piece above, left a great negative shape, which was used to print with the Gelli-Plate.

Cutting unusual fabrics

We tried mountboard, copper, different weights of Vilene, including a thick craft Vilene, and Heat'n'Bond cotton, which can be tricky to cut. The thick fusible craft Vilene cut really well. We have all used that a lot in this section.

> Copper shim cut with the Scan N Cut machine before being heat-coloured.

∧ The heat-coloured copper was embedded in many layers of melted embossing powder on distressed felt.

∧ A tree design cut from craft Vilene. This cut-out tree design has been stitched and is shown on the right.

> A drawing of a tree cut out of heavyweight craft Vilene which has an adhesive backing. It has been coloured with Lumiere paint and bonded to a backing of Stewart Gill Glitterati fibres on felt.

∧ Drawings and stencils cut on the Scan N Cut.

∧ Four small Scan N Cut stencils were placed on painted calico. Black acrylic paint was then applied to accentuate the negative shapes.

Stencils and masks

One very obvious use for the machines is the possibilities that they offer for making stencils. So often, we cut these laboriously by hand, only to be disappointed by the results when we come to use them. Most of the machines handle the stencil-making materials well and cut them cleanly. We have tried a good variety but those used most for the stencil work shown here are Art Van Go Stencil Acetate and Stix2 Clear Extra Thick Acetate sheets.

It is always worth looking at negative shapes for stencil-making. The shapes cut as positives often produce exciting options when the remaining material is examined and, best of all, they will relate really well to the positive shapes – so keep a close eye on the remnants.

When planning the design for stencils, all the usual rules apply. Remember that areas will be cut away, so include bridges where necessary to make sure that it all holds together. This is where the cutter has such a big advantage as you can experiment by cutting your design from paper and checking that it all works well.

∧ Paula's 'ghost' prints are made by saturating the pages of a sketchbook with fluid paint. Use two or three colours and just lay the die-cut card shapes and their negative shapes on top of the wet paint, close the book and allow to dry.

∨ Maggie's pressure stencils. An acetate stencil was cut on the Scan N Cut and placed on painted silk while the fabric was still wet. A few weights were placed on top and it was then left to dry.

Linking stencilled backgrounds to a theme

The ability to link backgrounds to foregrounds was discussed earlier and here it is illustrated with a technique that Paula calls 'ghost printing' and Maggie calls 'pressure stencils'. Both work in a similar way in that the background, be it paper or fabric, is painted with a fairly liquid paint and a shape – either a stencil or a positive shape – is laid on top and allowed to remain there until the paint dries. It can then be removed and will have left an imprint behind. Paula has produced some wonderful effects in her sketchbooks by drawing into these marks.

Maggie's version works best on fabric and calls for a stencil or positive shape cut from acetate or acrylic film. As before, the surface should be quite wet and this can be achieved by damping the fabric and then painting with silk paints or Brusho. Before it has a chance to dry, place the stencil on top and then put weights on one or two areas. The paint will be darker where it is exposed to the air but a certain amount of pattern is lost where the weights are placed. It produces a fabric that is suitable for any technique if heat-set when dry. It is also great when the scale of the motif is changed and the original is stitched on top.

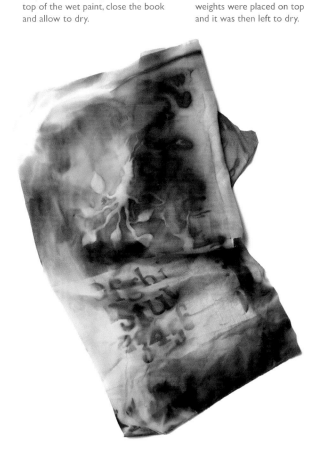

Working to a theme

We have seen how useful the option to produce cut versions of your own designs can be and the real test of this is to complete a good-sized piece of work based on shapes produced with the electronic cutter. Our loan machine was a Brother Scan N Cut, so we will be using that as we step through some of the stages to show you how we worked our themes. The machine itself is very straightforward to operate but, if you have a different machine, you should easily find the appropriate commands. We hope, however, that you will work to your own design source.

< Collagraph plate and
  print of a hare.

Theme one: Hares

Paula has long had a fascination for the hare, which is reflected in much of her work. Her sketchbooks were full of suitable designs, ideal for the scanner. Here, she has used the hare motif as inspiration for a series of stencils and a stitched piece cut from felt, all produced on the Scan N Cut.

The theme was then adapted for the Scan N Cut by making a clear black pen sketch and scanning it in.

This stencil has been very useful, on surfaces ranging from paper and fabric to leaves stuck to a sketchbook page.

∧ Leaves applied to tissue paper with Bondaweb. It was stencilled with black acrylic.

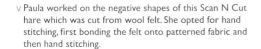

∨ Paula worked on the negative shapes of this Scan N Cut hare which was cut from wool felt. She opted for hand stitching, first bonding the felt onto patterned fabric and then hand stitching.

Moving into fabric Paula cut the hare shape from wool felt. This gave an excellent positive and negative shape. Keeping the negative shape she passed the positive on to Sam and you can see the results in the photographs.

∧ Sam's Scan N Cut hare used the positive shape cut from the wool felt. This was mounted onto hand-dyed fabric and machine-stitched using Wonderfil and Superior Threads.

< Sketchbook and materials
based on Wood Warriors.

Theme two: The Wood Warriors

Maggie's theme was based on an invented race
of fearsome beings – the Wood Warriors – who
lived long ago in deep woodland. Part of the
mythology concerned the masks worn by the
warriors, who often represented themselves as
animals. A drawing of a lion was made and, as it
was a symmetrical shape, only one side needed
to be drawn. It was then scanned into the Scan
N Cut, digitised, copied and flipped to form the
right side of the face.

< Drawing of one side of lion mask. It was scanned, copied
and flipped to achieve a symmetrical shape.

With the mask construction in mind, she drew two long curved sections below the chin which were designed to lock into place and push the mask outwards. The theme was pursued, as follows:

1. The lion drawing was scanned into the Scan N Cut and three lion shapes were cut from craft Vilene.

2. The three masks were sponged with cold tea and then coloured with Coloursoft pencils before acrylic wax was brushed over them.

3. The masks were hand-stitched before being mounted on a background made from a pressure stencil of lettering – giving the effect of old text.

4. A border was formed from heavyweight Vilene (the negative shape left over from a lettering die). The centre was removed.

5. When complete, holes bored in the centre of the mount, beneath the shapes, allowed cords from the stitched piece to pass through and tie on the reverse.

∧ Lion masks on heavyweight Vilene.

The shape worked so well that it suggested further three-dimensional options. The size of the lion mask was increased using the resize function and the four cut shapes were made into a bowl. Craft Vilene and gesso were coloured with inks and spray paints.

By now the 3D bug had really bitten and a piece of birch bark was cut to provide a groove for a backing panel made from a pressure stencil of the lion shape. Smaller grooves in the foreground allowed for some trees and foliage to soften the image and add perspective.

The mythology of the Wood Warrior tribe was explored further through a series of drawings and sketchbook trials based on the face shapes of the warriors. These drawings were scanned into the Scan N Cut and cut from craft Vilene, paying careful attention to the cutting lines, so that both positive and negative shapes could be used.

∧ Stencils were made from the lion drawing and stylised trees. Pressure was applied to produce the backdrop for this piece which also incorporates trees cut from craft Vilene.

∧ Lion Bowl after colouring and stitching together.

This piece had a base of birch bark but it could also be constructed from driftwood or interesting sticks picked up on a walk. Holes were drilled so that cords could be threaded through to hold the structure together. Sticks could be tied into a ladder with cords or string. The cords here were made by zigzagging over heavy yarns.

Then leaves were cut out, using Sizzix Tattered Leaf dies, from a variety of fabrics including metal.

Other leaves were cut from Vilene and decorated with gesso and were then attached to more machine-wrapped cords. Some of these had been fringed by laying the cord on water-soluble fabric and working straight lines over the top. The water-soluble fabric was then washed away. Finally, they were draped to fall through and along the birch bark structure and the heads of the warriors were displayed, tucked within the foliage.

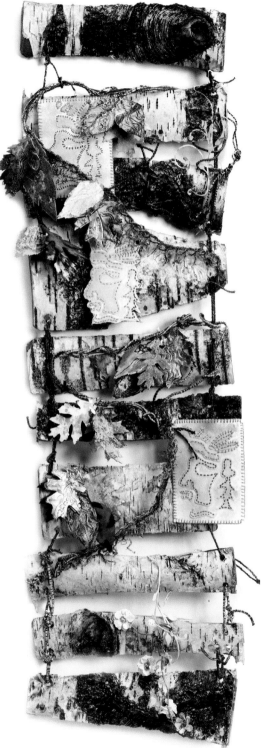

∧ Wood Warriors on bark strips.

> Wood Warriors made into bunting. Cut-out interior shapes glued to a painted Vilene background.

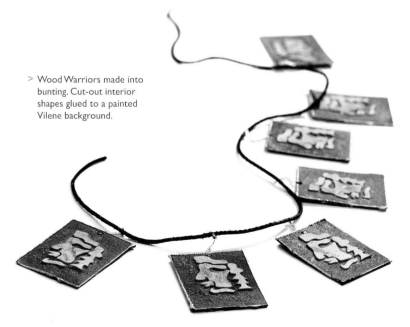

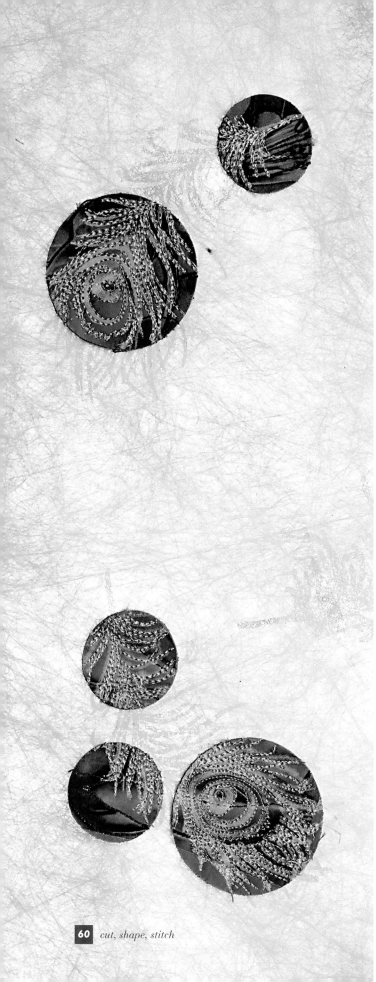

Theme three: Feathers

Sam has long used feathers in her work, appreciating their shape and the ability of the motif to become a fluffy, light design element or a more solid shape. Her previous work has included commercial stencils and Thermofax screens, combining these with die cut shapes, so she was excited by the option of making her own designs using the Scan N Cut.

This cape began with a drawing of a feather which she had already used to make a series of stencils. Drawn with black ink on paper, it was a very suitable candidate for scanning. With this design fixed to a mat, it was scanned into the Scan N Cut and the size was manipulated many times to make it as big and as small as the machine would allow (and many in between). Numerous stencils were cut, in all the sizes that had been created on the machine and layers of fabric were stencilled, some with gesso and some with molding paste. They were then stitched together.

The largest feather design was then cut on the machine from craft Vilene. This was painted with a mixture of black gesso and Xpandaprint and sprinkled with WOW Embossing Powder in Silver and Platinum. It was heated carefully with a heat tool. Other large feathers were created by stencilling black gesso onto Lutradur and heating the edges with a heat tool. The shapes were stitched onto the cape using Kreinik Fashion Twist in Carbon which has flecks of silver in it.

Further small feathers were cut out in craft Vilene and sprayed with Adirondack Color Wash Spray in Denim. These were sprinkled with blue embossing powder and heated before being applied to the neck edge. The outer edges of the cape were softened by using the craft Vilene negative shapes.

We're sure you have loads of design ideas that will translate into reality with the use of digital cutters, and hope that you will be able to lay your hands on one of the machines to try them out.

< Die-cut roundels with machine embroidery on computer-printed cotton, with a feather Thermofax screen. The round shapes were bonded to the fabric and the shape of a feather was free-machined over them and into the backing Lutradur fabric, also printed with the feather design.

> Feather masks cut from acetate in different sizes to show a change of scale. You can see the design for this above.

∨ Cape created using black sateen fabric, Soft and Stable stabiliser, with crash as a top layer. Feathers of varying sizes were created on the Scan N Cut and used as stencils and masks, together with craft Vilene cut-outs, decorated with ink sprays and embossing powder.

SECTION 4
Negative shapes

Really exciting things happen to the background fabric when the cut-outs have been made. This is particularly apparent when cutting anything with an intricate or jagged edge. When we were working on this book, we found ourselves getting just as excited about the bits we were throwing away as we were about the cuts we were making.

As suggested in Section 2, when you are cutting lots of shapes for a project – or even when cutting a series of shapes for different pieces – get into the habit of cutting a long strip, the width of your die cutter, and examine it after each session to see what can be gleaned from it. The vessels shown here were just offcuts from a long cutting strip that curled into beautiful shapes when I stood them on end.

^ Negative shape that resulted from cutting Sizzix Tattered Leaves and Florals from craft Vilene.

< This negative shape was painted with transfer paints, curled into a shape and stitched to hold it there. Very light seeding stitch in gold thread provided all that was needed for decoration.

> Negative of a flourish die-cut from folded fabric. It was placed on printed fabric and made into a small bag. The closures are made from wrapped pipe cleaners.

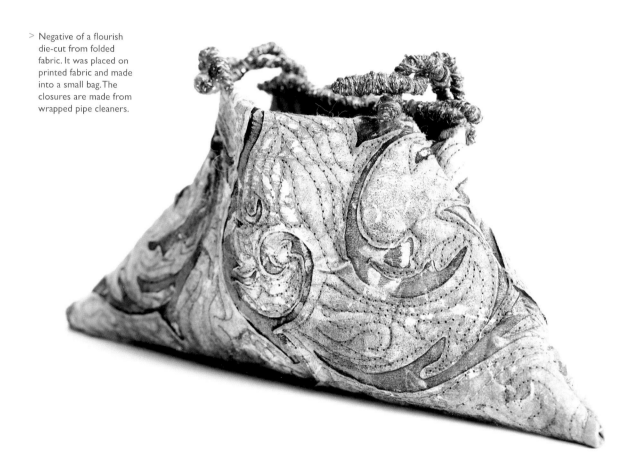

This bag was created from the negative shapes which resulted from cutting with the Elegant Flourish dies that were used on the cape on page 22. The painted Lutradur had been folded to cut the shapes and left a beautiful pattern behind. This was bonded to dark fabric and further enhanced with Markal Paintstiks in the negative shapes to intensify the blue colour.

Soft and Stable was used as a stabiliser which created a firm shape for the bag and allowed decorative machine embroidery over the surface. It was made into a bag and a closure was formed with pipe cleaners that had been wrapped in a toning yarn. The wrapping was increased towards the end of the pipe cleaners to produce finials.

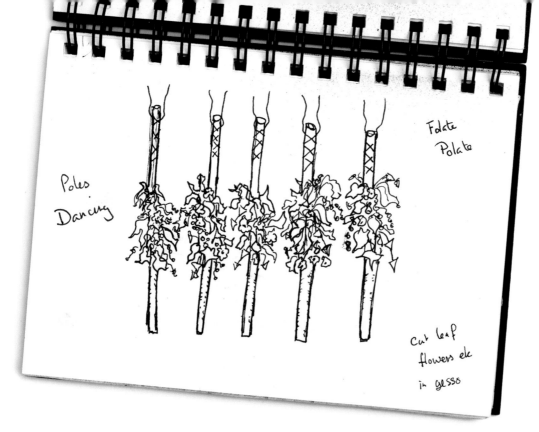

Poles
Dancing

Poles.
Dancing

Folate
Polate

Cut leaf
flowers etc
in gesso

< Rough sketch for *Poles Dancing*. The poles hang loosely and move (or dance) in the breeze.

> *Poles Dancing* – flowery maypoles designed to dance in the breeze.

Poles Dancing

These flowery 'danglies' came into being when I was cutting Tattered Florals and Tattered Leaves for the Metaphor piece in Section 2. The flowers and leaves were cut from narrow strips of craft Vilene and these strips formed very interesting negative shapes.

Poles Dancing, so called because the light bamboo supports sway in the slightest breeze, came about through experiments with the positive and negative shapes. The idea of garlands came to mind and the negative shapes were ideal for the central spiral. The spikey effect was just the thing to act as a contrast to the blowsy shapes of the blooms.

First, a supporting strip of craft Vilene was cut and 'garden-weight' wire was satin stitched to this, using a wide zigzag on the sewing machine. Then the strips of jagged shapes were machined to the outside.

The ends of the strips were snipped to a point and both sides were painted in bright colours with acrylic paint.

The flower shapes were a mix of felt and craft Vilene; both had silk bonded to the right side. They were cut with the Tattered Florals and Leaves dies, making more negative shapes.

Both flowers and leaves were sprayed with water to dampen the surface. They were then sprayed with silk paints, which mingled well on the damp surface. Finally, they were stitched to the central garland, wound around painted bamboo and attached to wrapped cords.

∨ Negative strip with wire inserted. Painted with acrylic paints.

Combining positive and negative shapes

Sometimes it is possible to combine the shapes and the offcuts in one piece. This journal page shows how the negative shapes were used to decorate the underlying page before being torn and pasted on top.

1. Cut strips of black card and die-cut shapes using the Memory Box Cottage Leaf die.

2. Paint the journal page with acrylic paint. Use the negative leaf void shape to stencil leaves all over the page with a variety of metallic paints. Use the positive leaf shapes in the same way to build up texture and colour.

3. The leaf shapes will also have built-up colour and texture. Stick these on one of the pages, massing them to make greater impact.

4. The strips of negative shapes will also have great texture and a build-up of colour. Tear the edges to expose the black card and form leaf shapes.

5. Collage together on the opposite page of the book.

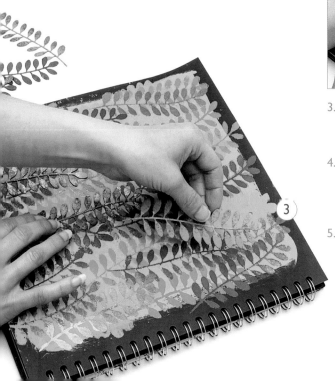

∧ Positive and negative pieces of a die-cut shape used to decorate a sketchbook page. Layering many layers of paint and collaging, the painted papers give this piece dimension and depth.

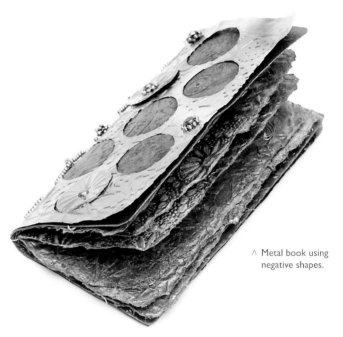

∧ Metal book using negative shapes.

Metal book

This metal-cutting technique is a great way of using both the positive and the negative – see page 26.

1. Cut the copper just a little larger than the size of the Sizzix circles die.

2. The copper negative shape with circles cut out is too good to waste.

3. Layer together the Vilene and copper and run through the machine in the embossing folder. If it is too big you can add hand embossing with an old ballpoint pen or pastry crimper.

4. Use a darning needle to make holes carefully in the middle of the copper circles.

5. Use an old ballpoint pen to score designs into the copper circles.

6. Pierce through the copper and Vilene to make guide holes for the brad pins and cog-shaped spacers. This will hold the layers together.

Now for something completely different

This intriguing piece was made from a cigar box, painted with acrylic paint. A Spellbinders Cherry Blossom die was used to cut branches for the lid of the box.

1. Aluminium shim, decorated with alcohol inks, was used to die-cut branches and small flowers that were glued to the surface.

2. The metal on the sides was formed from the negative shapes from the branches and flowers. Spellbinders make tiny dies to cut shapes that will fit perfectly into their bezels for use with resins.

3. The interior was filled with these bezels, together with jewellery findings and embossed metal. A hole was cut in the back of the box so that a battery-operated tealight could be inserted.

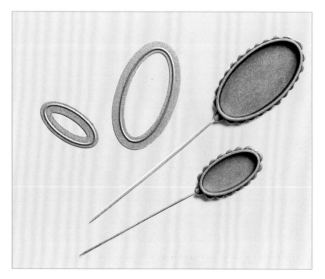

∧ A re-purposed cigar box
was decorated with negative
shapes cut from metal.

Stencilling from negative shapes

The negative shapes are wonderful for stencils. We have seen these stencils throughout the book, adding interest to background fabrics, but they are pretty good used for any form of surface decoration. The one shown here was made using the Gelli Plate.

When cutting stencils and masks (particularly with the digital machines), the line between positive and negative becomes blurred. Either can be used effectively for printing and the Gelli Plate lends itself to creating some vibrant printed pieces. Where circles are cut out, the negative space provides a stencil for creating random patterns while, with feathery tendrils, the lines ebb and flow along the edges of the printed surface.

Combining stencils and masks creates interesting patterns and the texture of the prints made from the plate ensures that you create unique pieces of work that you can rarely replicate. Where masks and stencils collect the paint and become a trifle blurred, they can be used for further 'ghost' prints. Offcuts from edges can create unusual lines that draw the eye to the print.

∧ Gelli-printed feather stencils.

We do hope you've found this book useful. We all agree that discovering the world of cut shapes has completely changed the way we work! Don't forget to go online to the d4daisy website **www.d4daisy.com**. You'll find lots more about cutters there.